Taxis

by Allison Lassieur

Consultant:
Allan Fromberg, Director of Public Affairs
New York Taxi and Limousine Commission

Bridgestone Books
an imprint of Capstone Press
Mankato, Minnesota

Bridgestone Books are published by Capstone Press
818 North Willow Street, Mankato, Minnesota 56001
http://www.capstone-press.com

Library of Congress Cataloging-in-Publication Data
Lassieur, Allison.
    Taxis/by Allison Lassieur.
    p. cm.—(The transportation library)
    Includes bibliographical references and index.
    Summary: Discusses the inventors, history, early models, major parts, and workings
of taxis.
    ISBN 0-7368-0365-3
    1. Taxicabs—Juvenile literature. [1. Taxicabs.] I. Title. II. Series.
HE5611.L274 2000
388.3'4232—dc21   99-24135
                                                                                    CIP

Editorial Credits
Karen L. Daas, editor; Timothy Halldin, cover designer and illustrator;
    Heather Kindseth, illustrator; Kimberly Danger, photo researcher

Photo Credits
Corbis, 12, 14–15, 16
David F. Clobes, 8
International Stock, 8 (inset); International Stock/Johnny Stockshooter, 6
James P. Rowan, 20
Photophile/J.R. & E.C. Stangler, cover
Victor Englebert, 18
Visuals Unlimited/John D. Cunningham, 4

Table of Contents

Taxis

Taxis are vehicles driven by taxi drivers. Taxi is short for taxicab. Taxis also are called cabs. People take taxis to travel short distances. Taxi drivers take passengers where they want to go. Many cities have taxis.

passenger
someone other than the driver who travels in a taxi or other vehicle

Traveling by Taxi

In some cities, people hail taxis from sidewalks. People sometimes phone for taxis. Taxis also may wait for people at airports and hotels. Passengers pay taxi drivers. The cost of a taxi ride depends on the distance the taxi travels.

hail
to get someone's attention;
people hail taxis so they will stop.

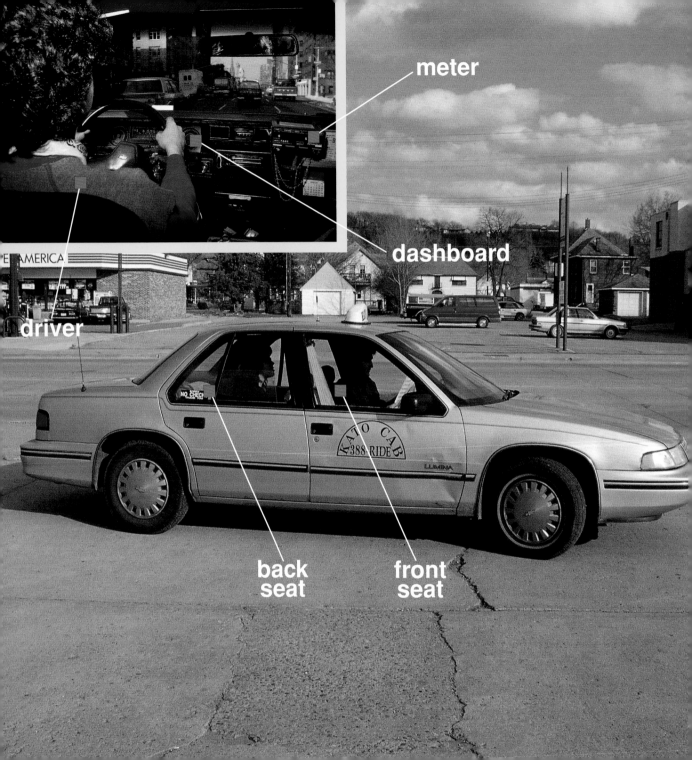

meter

dashboard

driver

back
seat

front
seat

Parts of a Taxi

A passenger usually sits in the back seat of a taxi. The driver sits in the front seat. A screen sometimes divides the back seat from the front seat. A meter on the dashboard shows the passenger how much the ride costs.

dashboard
the instrument panel of a car; gauges and warning lights are located on the dashboard.

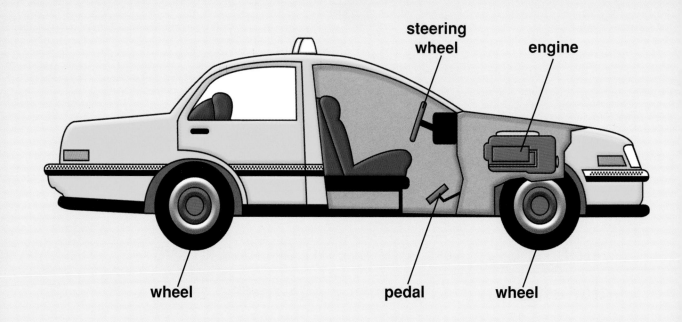

steering wheel

engine

wheel

pedal

wheel

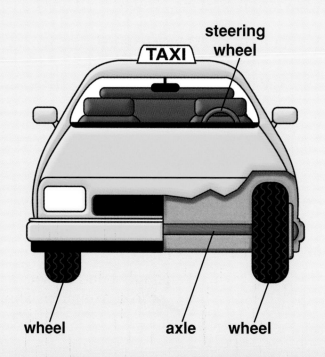

steering wheel

TAXI

wheel

axle

wheel

How a Taxi Works

Many taxis have a gas engine. Gas fuels the engine. The power from the engine moves the axles. The axles turn the wheels. A driver uses pedals on the floor to control the taxi's speed. A driver uses the steering wheel to turn the taxi.

axle
a rod in the center of a wheel; axles turn wheels.

Before the Taxi

People in cities walked or rode
horses before taxis were invented. But
walking was slow. Some people had
horse-drawn carriages. But carriages
were expensive. Not everyone could
afford to own a carriage.

Inventor of the Taxi

In 1891, Wilhelm Bruhn invented the taximeter. This machine showed how far carriages traveled. Soon taximeter cabs began service in Europe. People paid fares to ride in these horse-drawn carriages. Taximeters told drivers how much to charge passengers.

Early Taxis

In 1907, engine-powered taxis began service. These early automobiles were hard to drive. Drivers had to use many levers to start and move the taxis. Taxis changed as people improved the automobile.

Taxis around the World

Most taxis in the United States and Europe are cars. In Thailand, some taxis are big pickup trucks. People in some countries ride in bicycle taxis or motorcycle taxis. Some countries have rickshaws. People pull these small carriages.

Taxi Facts

- Taxis in London, England, are called black cabs. But not all black cabs are black. They can be different colors.

- All New York City taxis have a special trouble light. Drivers can secretly turn on the light if they have problems. Police officers see the trouble light and help the drivers.

- Taxis in some cities run on natural gas. This fuel pollutes the air less than gasoline.

- In some cities, taxi drivers must go to school to get a taxi driver's license.

- Some taxis have a light on the roof. The light tells people if the taxi is available.

Hands On: Wheels and Axles

A taxi's engine powers axles. Axles turn the wheels on the taxi. Axles also make wheels more steady. You can learn how wheels and axles work.

What You Need
Scissors
Tagboard or cardboard
Paper punch
Drinking straw

What You Do
1. Cut two small circles out of tagboard or cardboard.
2. Punch a hole in the center of each circle. Each circle is a wheel. Try rolling one wheel on a table. It will fall over.
3. Put the drinking straw through the hole in the middle of each wheel. One wheel should be at each end of the straw. The straw acts as an axle.
4. Push the straw forward. The two wheels roll together when an axle connects them.

The movement of the axle makes the wheels turn.

Words to Know

carriage (KA-rij)—a vehicle with wheels that is usually pulled by horses

engine (EN-juhn)—a machine that makes the power needed to move something

fare (FAIR)—the cost of traveling in a taxi

meter (MEE-ter)—a machine that keeps track of how much money a taxi ride costs

pollute (puh-LOOT)—to make dirty

rickshaw (RIK-shaw)—a small carriage that is usually pulled by a person

Read More

Graham, Ian. *Cars, Bikes, Trains, and Other Land Machines.* How Things Work. New York: Kingfisher Books, 1993.
Wilson, Anthony. *On the Move: A Visual Timeline of Transportation.* New York: DK Publishing, 1995.

Internet Sites

Automotive Learning On-line
http://www.InnerAuto.com/Default.htm
New York City Taxi and Limousine Commission
http://www.ci.nyc.ny.us/taxi
Transportation Wonderland
http://education.dot.gov/k5/gamk5.htm

Index